Kid Pick!

Title: _____

Author: _____ 07

Picked by: _____

_____

Why I love this book:

_____

_____

Wild Colors

Photography by
GAVRIEL JECAN
Text by
ANDREA HELMAN

Introduction by ART WOLFE

SASQUATCH BOOKS
SEATTLE

Introduction

What is color? A scientist would say there are no colors, only light waves of different lengths being reflected from objects. But as a photographer for more than thirty years, I know it is one of the most—if not THE most—critical factor in my work. It is an important tool in visual communication, with a direct link to emotion and behavior. Color is not just what we see with the naked eye, but also what we feel: happiness, contentment, anger, and fear. Interpreting that through photography is an exciting challenge.

In nature, the range of color is truly glorious and adeptly utilized. Many animals use color to blend in with their surroundings while others use it as a warning of danger. Both plants and animals use color as an attraction device, for critical pollination, and courtship. Without color where would we be? Life would be dull indeed.

Color is deceptive. From afar, forests appear as a study of grays and blues. But walk under the canopy and those colors vaporize before the innumerable shades of lush green and velvety brown. In the Amazon rainforest there are the most colorful species in the world: poison arrow frogs, scarlet macaws, golden tamarins, and iridescent butterflies.

As documented by photographer Gavriel Jecan and writer Andrea Helman, color in nature is diverse and fascinating. I invite you to journey around the world and explore the world of Wild Colors!

—Art Wolfe

CHARTREUSE

Western Tiger Swallowtail Caterpillar

The spooky yellow eyes of the western tiger swallowtail caterpillar aren't really eyes at all, but eyespots, or fake eyes meant to scare away predators. The caterpillar lines a leaf with silk, folds it over, and ties it up around itself for feeding and shelter. Soon, the creepy caterpillar will turn into a beautiful butterfly with black tiger-striped wings.

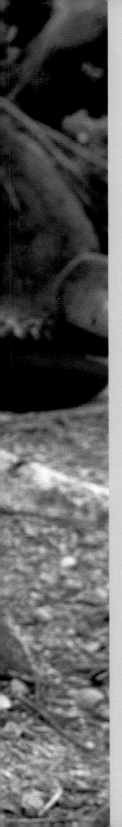

BLUE

Blue-Footed Booby

While clumsy on land, the blue-footed booby can catch flying fish in midair and, from high above the water, dive headfirst beneath the waves with barely a splash! When courting, a male booby proudly parades about, displaying his bright blue feet and then flashing them at his mate in a courtship flight. The broad webbed feet also keep the baby eggs warm until they hatch. Then the chicks sit on their parents' feet until they are one month old.

BLACK and WHITE

———— Zebra

Zebras wander the African grasslands looking for the next water hole. But in the surrounding tall grass, the lions are looking for zebras. No two zebras look the same. Like your fingerprint, each pattern is different. A zebra's stripes are dazzling to the eye and disguise its shape from predators. Zebras like to be together barking and braying in conversation and loyally protecting the weakest family member.

LAVENDER

Lavender

Every summer the soothing scent of lavender fills the air and colors the hills of Provence, France. Most of the flowers are picked by machine, but some fields are still picked by hand. Lavender has been used for perfume and soap, aches and pains, bruises and bites, and even to tame lions and tigers!

SILVER

Sockeye Salmon

After years at sea, silvery sockeye salmon make the dangerous trip back to their Alaskan river home. Hungry bears and other fish are after them. Up! They jump over waterfalls, traveling many miles upriver to the very stream where they were born, and lay their eggs. For two million years, this has been their life cycle.

BROWN

Impala

Graceful grazing impalas are never far from a soothing drink of water. But when disturbed, the glossy brown herd jumps straight up in the air. Up and down, zig and zag, leaping over each other! This crisscross explosion of color confuses the predator and makes it hard to single out one impala.

GREEN

and

RED

Red-Eyed Tree Frog

The red-eyed tree frog starts life brown then changes from light green to dark green or reddish brown, depending on his mood! Sticky, orange suction toe-pads and strong, long blue legs keep him climbing, hopping, and hanging on to leaves, branches, and the sides of trees. In the rainforest, green helps him stay hidden during the day, but should a predator appear? Pop! He opens his brilliant red eyes and startles it away.

GRAY

Koala

They look like bears, but koalas are related to kangaroos and when born are no bigger than a jellybean. Their gray, woolly, waterproof coat blends well with eucalyptus tree bark. Koalas love the strong bitter eucalyptus leaves, but to us they would taste like cough drops! Feeding at night, the fuzzy koala happily wedges itself into a tree limb, nods off while still chewing, then sleeps most of the day.

RED

Blood Starfish

"Danger!" says the vivid red color of the blood starfish. A clam is doomed in its powerful grip. Pop! The shell is opened and the starfish eats a clam dinner. A starfish's feet have thousands of small suction cups helping it move around. If it loses an arm, another grows back.

CLEAR

Dragonfly

The zippy dragonfly comes in many colors, including clear. It is the oldest and one of the fastest flying insects on Earth. With great speed and acrobatics, it catches insects in midair, escapes from predators, and uses its bristled legs like a basket, trapping prey and returning to a favorite perch to eat. Dragonflies are always on the move—forward, backward, darting, diving, and resting only for a second.

Lesser Flamingos

Living where there is lots of mud and water, the lesser flamingos of Africa love to lap up algae. Their positively pink plumage and red eyes come from the plants they eat which contain carotene. You eat carotene in carrots. When the fluffy flamingos take off, they balance their long legs by flying with an outstretched neck.

BLACK

Black Bear

The smallest bears in North America, black bears are the least aggressive and not always black—sometimes this species is brown or white. But they are always hungry. Black bears love honey, nuts, berries, insects, and splashing about in streams catching a rich salmon dinner. If a ripe piece of fruit is out of reach, they just stand on their hind legs and grab it.

WHITE

Polar Bear

Deep in a snowdrift den, a female polar bear gives birth to twins who stay with mom for three years. A thick, white, waterproof coat keeps the polar bear warm and dry, blends well with the snowy arctic landscape and, in water, helps the hungry hunter appear like a chunk of floating ice. Sometimes, the polar bear covers his black nose with a large padded paw to make himself even more invisible!

17

TURQUOISE

Stinkbug

Phooey! Who disturbed the stinkbug? This stinkbug keeps predators away with its strong stinky odor and bright color. Stinkbugs are also called shield bugs because the female uses her body to shield the eggs she lays in tight rows on leaves, twigs, or around a plant stem.

GREEN

Cryptic Katydid

In the tropical rainforests of South America, the cryptic katydid rubs its wings together and sings out loudly through the still night air. Katydids love leaves and spend their lives on the plants they eat. They fool predators by mimicking, or imitating, the leaves they love.

ORANGE

Cup Fungus

In the life of the rainforest, this little fungus plays a big role. Feeding off of downed logs, branches, and leaves, it puts nutrients back into the soil. Without it, the forest would be buried under piles of leaves and branches. So, the small fungus is one of the earth's biggest recyclers—and a good source of food when roasted or boiled in banana leaves.

TAN

Lion

Lions are social animals, rubbing heads together to say, "Hello!" But in the African savanna, lions are the biggest, baddest cats around. The lion's tan coat hides it well in the tawny, tall African grassland, an effective camouflage while on the hunt for zebras. Lions live in family groups called "prides." Together, they hunt, guard their territory, and raise their young. They locate each other and call to their cubs with a loud ROAR!

BLACK and ORANGE
———
Monarch Butterfly

Traveling farther than any butterfly on Earth, millions of monarch butterflies fly thousands of miles each winter to southern mountain forests. Following the exact same route each year, they roost in the exact same trees, covering them like a colorful carpet. Their colors are a warning to birds and mice to stay away. Predators avoid the monarch because it tastes bad—and they avoid the viceroy butterfly because it looks like a monarch!

RAINBOW

Keel-Billed Toucan

All colors of the rainbow, except violet, can be found in the bills of different toucans. The bill's colors and patterns help each bird recognize one another and find a mate. Large and light, the bill is almost as long as the toucan's body. With its sharp tip, the toucan snips off a tasty treat of juicy fruit, tosses its head back and—plop!—swallows it whole.

RUST

Bornean Orangutan

Shy and solitary, orangutans are very caring mothers. Babies stay with mom for three years or until she has another child. Using their powerful arms, legs, and agile fingers, the rusty-colored orangutan swings quickly through the treetops and appears to vanish into the dense forest. Considered one of the most intelligent of land animals, they weave branches together for a springy bed, crack open tough coconuts, and memorize the best routes for finding food.

MAGENTA and GOLD

Sea Anemone

Beware of this beautiful "flower of the sea." It's a predatory animal! What appear to be "petals" are really stinging tentacles surrounded by a large mouth. Attached to coral or rocks, the sea anemone awaits an unsuspecting fish. Zap! Chomp! The prey is stung and eaten by the colorful creature. Sea anemones come in many shapes, sizes, and colors and use their stunning sting for food, defense, and to protect other animals of the sea.

Thick-Tailed Scorpion

Burrowing beneath the gritty South African sand, the thick-tailed scorpion uses its tail to dig out hiding places near shrubs or under rocks. H-I-S-S! the scorpion warns. The thick tail is held above its head, ready to strike a defensive jab or inject poisonous venom. After dinner is caught, the scorpion enjoys it very slowly … sometimes spending as long as one hour on a single juicy beetle!

BLUE and YELLOW
Macaw

Nesting high above the rainforest floor, the blue and yellow macaw peeks out of its comfortable tree cavity. At dawn, flocks leave their roosts and fly great distances to feed and bask in the warm sun, perfectly blending in with the sunlight and blue sky. A member of the parrot family, the macaw has a piercing loud scream and the strongest bite in the bird world.

29

BLACK and TAN

Cheetah

Built for speed, cheetahs are fast-moving machines. Over short distances they can zip along at 75 miles per hour—as fast as cars on the highway—making them the fastest animals on Earth. In the grass, the cheetah's spots camouflage it, and a white tip at the end of the female's tail helps cubs follow mom. She calls them with a CHURP! and PURRS loudly while washing and feeding them.

YELLOW and PURPLE
Crab Spider

Unlike most spiders, patient crab spiders, on Earth for 300 million years, don't weave webs to catch their food. They might hide for weeks inside a flower and, with one fatal bite, seize a bee or butterfly dropping by for a sip of sweet nectar. The clever crab spider hangs extra prey below its hiding place and can change colors to match the flower or leaf it's hiding on.

For Art Wolfe and the Art Wolfe Inc. staff—thank you for everything you have done for me. —GJ.

For mom, a class act, with never a hue out of place
and Dad, who always brightens my world, inspires and teaches by example to color outside the lines.
For Gavriel, who made it possible, and bear hugs to the clan in the Wolfe den. —A.H.

Printed in Hong Kong
Published by Sasquatch Books
Distributed by Publishers Group West
10 09 08 07 06 05 04 03   6 5 4 3 2 1

Cover & interior design: Kate Basart
Cover & interior photographs: Gavriel Jecan
Copy editor: Amy Novesky

Library of Congress Cataloging in Publication Data
Helman, Andrea.
Wild colors / by Andrea Helman ; photographs by Gavriel Jecan.
p. cm.
Summary: Photographs of exotic animals and plants present a wide array of colors.
ISBN 1-57061-391-5
1. Color—Pictorial works—Juvenile literature. [1. Color. 2. Nature.] I. Jecan, Gavriel, ill. II. Title.
QC495.5.H47 2003
535.6—dc21   2003052802

Sasquatch Books
119 South Main Street, Suite 400
Seattle, WA 98104
206/467-4300
www.sasquatchbooks.com
books@sasquatchbooks.com

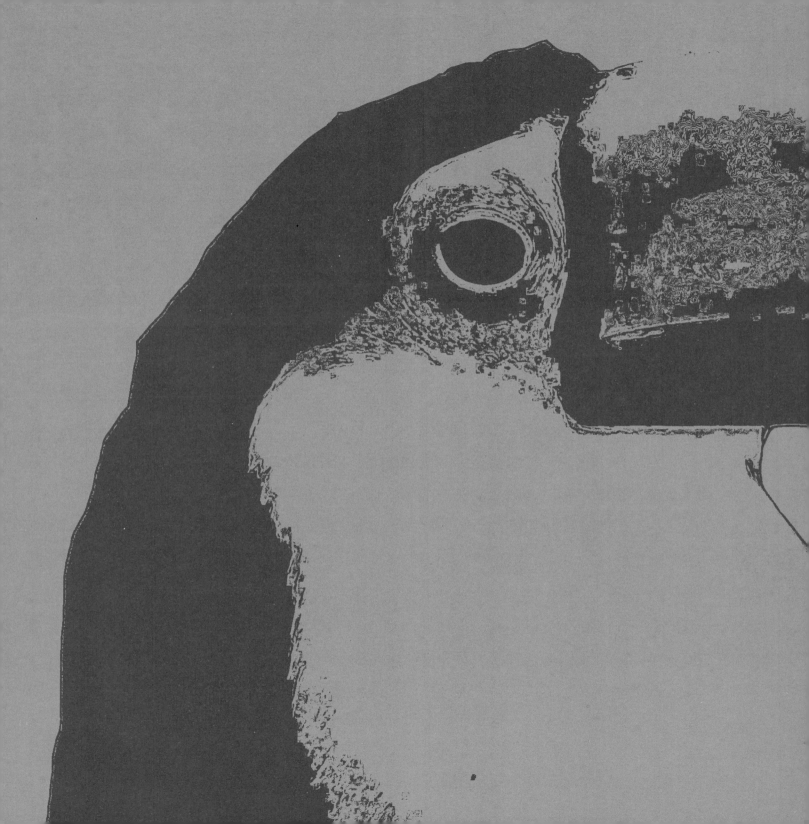